# The Upward Look

Including The Book Formerly Published
Under The Title, "Golden Rule
Meditations," With Prayers For Each Day
Of A Month

By

Amos R. Wells

*First Fruits Press*
*Wilmore, Kentucky*
*c2015*

*The upward look: including the book formerly published under the title, "Golden rule meditations," with prayers for each day of a month,* by Amos R. Wells.

First Fruits Press, ©2015
Previously published: Boston and Chicago: United Society of Christian Endeavor, ©1903.

ISBN: 9781621713999 (print), 9781621714002 (digital)

Digital version at http://place.asburyseminary.edu/christianendeavorbooks/23/

First Fruits Press
B.L. Fisher Library
Asbury Theological Seminary
204 N. Lexington Ave.
Wilmore, KY 40390
http://place.asburyseminary.edu/firstfruits

Wells, Amos R. (Amos Russel), 1862-1933.
    The upward look : including the book formerly published under the title, "Golden rule meditations," with prayers for each day of a month / by Amos R. Wells.
    Iv, 138 pages ; 21 cm.
    Wilmore, Ky. : First Fruits Press, ©2015.
    Reprint. Previously published: Boston : United Society of Christian Endeavor, ©1903.
    ISBN: 9781621713999 (pbk.)
    1. Conduct of life -- Religious aspects -- Christianity. I. Title.
BJ1571 .W332 2015

Cover design by Jonathan Ramsay

asburyseminary.edu
800.2ASBURY
204 North Lexington Avenue
Wilmore, Kentucky 40390

*First Fruits*
THE ACADEMIC OPEN PRESS OF ASBURY SEMINARY

First Fruits Press
*The Academic Open Press of Asbury Theological Seminary*
204 N. Lexington Ave., Wilmore, KY 40390
859-858-2236
first.fruits@asburyseminary.edu
asbury.to/firstfruits

# THE UPWARD LOOK

INCLUDING THE BOOK FORMERLY PUB-
LISHED UNDER THE TITLE, "GOLDEN
RULE MEDITATIONS," WITH PRAYERS
FOR EACH DAY OF A MONTH

By AMOS R. WELLS

BOSTON AND CHICAGO
The United Society of Christian Endeavor

# CONTENTS

iv CONTENTS

# 1

## ON SABBATHS

HOW beautiful is this Sabbath day! Spirits of rest brood in the heavens and walk about the earth. Something is missing from my shoulders; it is the burden of yesterday. My mind, yesterday so oppressed with cares, forgets even what load has been lifted. I have not planned for this peace. God, far back in the creation, and through all the wise ordering of the ages, has been preparing it for me. God has thrust it upon me, though yesterday I should have rejected it to continue my tasks. Ah! why has he not forced upon me a continual Sabbath? Indeed, may I not have it? These bird-songs are the same as Saturday. Saturday's sunshine was as holy, air as clear, and trees as gracious. The Sabbath has come within me, for God and his world keep Sabbath all the time. Yield me the secret, O Father, by which thou dost carry on works so mighty with such abiding peacefulness. Let me teach my tasks to sing a Sabbath anthem with me. Let me teach my heart to cease from fretting on thy Sabbath days. Here on earth let me begin the Sabbath of eternity, whose toil is fruitful because it is untroubled, whose rest is perfect because it sings with labor. Draw me, Father of Sabbaths, close to thee and to thy peace.

# II

## ON UNDESERVED LOVE

MY loved ones love me as if I deserved their love. It is poured out unearned, slighted, and even rebuked. It is so great that a little kindness satisfies it, and it goes on. It is so foolish that it even transforms my faults into virtues, and sees something to love in all my ugliness. What angers others only pains my loved ones ; and the evil in me that others do not try to forget, they do not even remember. Or do they hide their pain when I slight them, as I afterwards hide my remorse and shame? and is their contentment with me partly feigned, like my carelessness? Let me cease to brood over such thoughts, that I may the more manfully make them impossible. O thou who dost see in all true disciples thy mother and sister and

3

brother, I cast upon thee all my burden of sin against my loved ones. Thy great love will fill up the great lack in mine. Thou wilt unburden me of the past, and thou wilt direct me into worthier ways. O thou who didst never cause a heart-ache, teach thy servant to love. O thou from whom affection never shrank abashed, teach thy servant to love. O thou who wert never too busy to be kind, teach thy servant to love. I will be taught of thee, and win myself from shame.

# III

## ON PALTRY SUCCESSES

I DID the best God then gave me to do, and felt depressed because God gave me no better. When shall I gain the healthy mind, the cheery spirit, that is triumphant when God works his will with me? Is not that to be illustrious enough? What matters it whether his will deals with my failures or my successes, with great deeds or petty deeds, so that it deals with me? It is more blessed to be used of God in small deeds than in great, because then I shall be sure that God honors me for myself and not for my works. It is better that the applause of men should be hushed, that in the silence I may hear God's approval. Would I have my patent of nobility signed by the scullion as well as by the king? Father, grant me the power to leave my work, after it is done, with thee and not with men. Father, I would have no rival to thy " Well done ! " Help me to such love for thee that I can spare men's praise. Nay, help me, Father, to such love for men that I can spare men's praise. What are we, that we should judge each other scornfully? Ah, what are we, that we should judge each other praisefully? Thou art the Judge, whether to exalt or depress. To thee alone we rise; from thee alone we fall; and not from men. Be thou so near me that, with all faithfulness to the world's work and all love for men, whether they love me or slight me, I may yet live to none but thee.

# IV

## ON A CROWDED LIFE

I AM troubled about my living. So much to do with power so slight, so many things with so little time, so sacred duties with so feeble inspiration. Requirement presses on requirement half accomplished, and the good keeps me so busy that I have no time to seek the better. Here and there, everywhere in my life, are loose ends, fragments of accomplishment. Nothing is beautifully finished. Nothing is rounded into solid usefulness. Some day will there not come a crash in all this ill-formed life of mine, tumbling it into fitting chaos? Creator, Father, shall I ever make myself what thou didst intend me? O forgive me, Father, that I forgot thou didst create me! O forgive me, Creator, that I forgot thy fatherhood! Thy creatures crowd space beyond space, but thy love reaches farther. The time whose limits oppress me, thou didst create. The small strength which thou didst give me is akin to thy great strength, and may summon it. Thou didst create me and thou dost love me. So firmly by those two strands is my life knit to thine that if, while I am doing my best, my life should tumble into ruin, it must draw thine infinite being with it. O, that what I thus know with my mind I may know with my heart! Assure me of thy presence with me in my work. Teach me to form my life by letting thee form it. Tenderly draw me out of my fretfulness into thy peace.

# V

## ON THE FEAR OF DEATH

WHY do I fear death for myself? It is not because I dread the pain of dissolution, for the pain of a toothache is often worse. It is not a shrinking from the darkness beyond, because Christ has made it all light to me, proving that God is good. It is not doubt of a happy heaven; I have not so known my Saviour. Nor is it always, though it often is, unwillingness to leave the fair expanse of earth, its joys but little tried, my work in it so poorly done; for I know that death can mean no narrowing of enjoyment, no break in any true undertaking. More often my fear of death is born of others' fear. My dear ones, how they grieve when loved ones die! What pitiful, white faces, and choking sighs, and black garb, true em-

9

blem of darkened lives! And I know
that, unworthy as I am of such love,
their sorrow would be long and deep for
me. So I fear death for myself because
I pity others ; yes, and I fear death for
others because I pity myself. Their
endless gain I count less than my few
years of loss. Their emancipation, their
exaltation, their enlargement, their riches
of life with the Lord, — a selfish tear dis-
solves it all from my memory. Why
cannot we be more brave, my loved ones
and I ? We are to live forever; why
should we love like ephemerals ? Why
should the short separation to come embitter with salt tears our dwelling together here ? To them and to me, O
Lord of death and of life, gracious Lord
of life and of death, grant the wisdom
that sees things truly, grant the courage
that knows but one Master, grant the
love that is serene forever, resting on
the arm of the undying One.

# VI

## ON MEN'S APPROVAL

YESTERDAY I was successful. I did my work swiftly and well, and won men's hearty praise. And then I worked the harder, and became still more successful, to win greater praise; but the praise did not come. Thereupon I became gloomy and discontented, and the lack of men's praise embittered all my work; so that I cried in anger, "What is the use of toiling for ungrateful men?" Thus I turned all my successes into failure, because I forgot that thou, O God, art my only success. And thus I turned all my accomplishment into ashes, because I forgot that thou, O Christ, art my only accomplishment — to win thy smile and thine indwelling. Will it be wrong if, in this coming day, I remember with joy as I work that men will praise me for it? Is it wrong to be pleased with any applause but thine? Thou wouldst not say so, for thou didst teach us to care for human love ; and men's approval is sweet because their love is sweet. Yet forgive me, Lord, because I have set men's love above thy matchless love, and have been disconsolate at missing this lesser love, as if the owner of a diamond mine should fret for a gravel bank. And as long as this praise of my brothers and sisters dulls my ears to thy whisper of warning or of blessing, grant that all human tongues may be chained from commendation, and all human hands held from applause.

# VII

## ON GOODS

POSSIBLY it was the roaring of the flame up the chimney ; or possibly it was the fire alarm which just sounded. For some cause, at any rate, my thoughts have turned to my dearest material possessions, my books. I doubt not others have goods as dear, — books likewise, or silks, or pictures, or gems, — but I wonder if they are so fearful for their treasures as I for mine. Here my books are, ranked before me in their kindly covers, old friends and trusty, every leaf heavy with golden memories. But a match in a luckless corner, or a faulty flue in my neighbor's house, and they would be gone, nor could all the world replace them. What should I do without them ? Ah, what shall I do without them, when I have done with material things, when

I go to the land of spirit? Yet how do I know that I must learn to do without them? Eye hath not seen nor mind conceived the joys the Father hath in store. But ah! those joys are for those who love him, and with the whole heart. Take, then, from my heart, O Giver of all good, whatever love of thy good things prevents supreme love of thee. Make me willing for the loss of all things, books, friends, home, all things, that I may find thee. Then, I know, I shall truly find all my possessions for the first time.

# VIII

## ON WORKING WITH OTHERS

IF one could only work alone! How annoying to have my plans pushed awry by the plans of others, my work left incomplete through the failure of their work, my zeal checked by their opposition! How difficult to have patience with the slow, to restrain the over-eager, to correct mistakes, to repeat careful instructions! Not only my time is lost, but my energy and spirit for work. There is discipline won in dealing with men, but might it not be won in easier ways? I may do them good, but how unkind in them to need my good offices! If I could work alone, every hindrance would be removed but my own faults, and every annoyance would cease but my own peevishness. Truly, these would be enough, without the peevishness and

faults of others. O my Master, when
thou wert on the earth, how didst thou
endure to work with men? Thou who
art perfect, with their imperfections;
and thou who art all-gracious, with their
gracelessness? When I remember how
thou didst say, " Father, forgive them,"
and how patient thou wert when thy disciples all forsook thee, I am ashamed
of my complaining. Do my friends, I
wonder, thus complain at my being with
them? Would they, too, prefer to work
alone? Grant me such gracious helpfulness, my Father, that they may never
have that thought of me; and such humility, that I may cease to have that
thought of them.

# IX

## ON PRAISE

O THAT my words were choirs, each choir of a thousand songs! Thanksgiving itself is graceless, and shamed by the truth. My days have been all ungrateful, and so must they be forever. Yet it is meet, my Father, to offer thee unmeet praise. Praise for the knowledge of thee, and for the assurance that it will grow constantly clearer. Praise that thou hast given me the secret of infinite years, hast taught me immortality. Praise for the hope of heaven. Praise for the translation of earth, its commonplace become marvels, its worries become calmness, its aches become promises. Praise for my tasks wherewith thou dost let me help thee in thy mighty labors. Praise for the dear delights of home and loved ones. Praise for the every-day blessings of sun and air and sky and soil, of warmth and shelter. Praise for books and a mind that can feed upon them. Praise for the Book that dwarfs all books. Praise for friends, for helpers, for lovers. And praise, praise, praise, for the friendship, the help, the mighty and wonderful love of Christ Jesus my Lord.

# X

## ON MANY BURDENS

HOW much I have to do to-day! And not only how much, but what a variety of things! Involved with my work, too, is the work of others, who may be lazy or incompetent, and whose fault may spoil my labor. And I must meet many people, the ill-natured, the mean, the debasing; and before all these men, and in all these trials, I must be calm and strong and cheery, illustrating the doctrine of my Lord. Surely my cares are many, and my tasks beyond my power to accomplish. Ah, foolish being that I am, I have nothing to do! Nothing to do, O Christ the toiler, because thou dost do it all; and no care to fret about, because thou carest for me. Forgive me because I go all thy sweet day through with phantoms of burdens weighing me down, fancying that I am bearing the load, when I bear only the semblance of it! Forgive me because I fret so many of thy sweet hours away, cowering before ghosts of cares whose real selves thou hast long ago put to flight! Forgive me, and pity me, because these unrealities seem often very real to me; and teach my eyes to see the truth. Keep me from conjuring up, with my pride of self, with my weak distrust of heaven, these brain-born worries and empty fears. In this calm morning meditation I am sure of thine upholding. Maintain, O Lord, that trust throughout the day.

# XI

## ON LONELINESS

NOW I go forth into the day alone. My dear ones are far away, and none but strangers about me. What do they know of my needs, my hopes, my fears? Yes, and what do I know of theirs? Kind people they may be, but how may I know of their kindness? Their wisdom and strength and beauty of soul are all, to a stranger, as if they were not. It is a sad thing to be alone in God's crowded world. In God's world! O Father, forgive me. Forgive me, thou Elder Brother, who wert deserted by all thy disciples! I remember now that thou wert lonely in order that no man henceforth need know loneliness; "that where thou art we may be also." I had forgotten that thou art with me. And I had not thought what

throngs thou bringest with thee ; for in
this great city how many thousands dwell
in thee, and with them I shall dwell daily
when I live in thee.  Why can I not feel
this, O my Father ?  Why do I ever deem
myself alone ?  Why do I not exult daily
and hourly in my riches of friends in
thee?  Something in my heart tells me
the reason, — tells me that I lack the
unselfish love which is thy passport into
thy kingdom of friends, where is no soli-
tude.  Help me to this love, my loving
Father, for I am tired of being alone.

# XII

## ON DEBTS

HOW much that is in my life for strength and joy is not my own, but the gift of others! Here I take daily credit for the exercise of abilities which others have chiefly developed, in ways of usefulness which others have opened to me. Subtract from my life what teachers and friends and books have put there, and surely the remnant would permit no pride. Touches of love, inspiration of example, the promptings of confidence reposed in me, prayers of God's saints, kindly counsel of my elders, — by a thousand daily happenings such as these, I am upheld and moved without my knowledge. Yes, and without my gratitude. For this, forgive me, revered teachers, loved friends, and friendly books. Forgive me, thou God of all upholding. When, in all thine eternal years, shall I have paid my debts, I who have not yet understood them ? Must I be bankrupt through ages of ages ? If it be thy will, O Lord. Thou didst make me weak, needing a world of helpers, that so I might learn the hill whence cometh the help of the world. I shall not be ashamed in thy great day though the good I have done to others be dwarfed by the good they have done to me, if this has been thy will for all. Perhaps the love even of a debtor may help to save mankind.

# XIII

## ON STUMBLINGS

DAILY and hourly, when I would be strong, I am weak. Falling into traps I have spread for myself, stumbling against obstacles I myself have reared, vainglorious yet despising myself, confident and headstrong under a dismal burden of failures that no one sees but God and his angels, — how dare I walk in these familiar paths? What assurance have I that where I have so often sinned I shall not sin again? My pride is the same, and my fall will be the same. And if I flee from the temptations that daily vanquish me, the very flight will bring me more completely under their sway. God will not be there more than here; nor will evil be less at another place or another time. A morning of good deeds will not save me from an afternoon of sin. My eyes fill with tears at the thought of my Saviour, and yet I pass from the story of his perfect years to a life all foul with selfishness. O Christ, thou knowest my frame, thou knowest why I fall ; I know not. I am not strong enough even to get from thee the help I need. Do thou press it on me. Take a tempted life that yields to sin, and force it to yield to thee. Lead me not into temptation ; deliver me from evil.

# XIV

## ON CONFESSING FAULTS

WHY do I always increase and
perpetuate my faults by my unwillingness to confess them? I cover
my shame and let it smoulder, instead of
bidding it consume openly before men's
eyes the dross that is in me. My rare
petitions for forgiveness have melted
my soul, have left me at peace; yet still
I shrink from the winning of this rest.
It is not hard to abase myself before
God; when no eye sees, save his, to
throw ashes on my head, and beat my
breast in despair and remorse. Why
should it be hard, then, to ask the pardon of God's creatures? Ah, I fear that
I think more of my offence toward men
than of my offence toward God; otherwise, it would be easy to confess to men,
but I should tremble to draw near the

throne of the Just One. Take from me, O merciful Judge, my shamefaced fear of the brother whom I have offended, and cause me to fear in shame the God whom I have much more offended. Thus I may more often ask my brother's forgiveness; thus I may less often need to seek in despondency the blessed forgiveness of my Lord.

# XV

## ON COMMONPLACE PEOPLE

MY conscience accuses me that I treated my acquaintance ill. Whatever the outward appearance, there was no heart of kindliness. And that was all because I thought the man commonplace. Are there, then, men in whom I dare be uninterested ? Men upon whom God has set his image, though it is marred and blurred, men of hopes and joys and fears, men who will live forever, — who am I, to call these commonplace ? What but one of the very common places of God's universe do I fill ? When my Lord was upon the earth, he did not attach himself to poets and deep thinkers, but to men of humdrum, ordinary lives. In that marvellous way he proved his divinity, by discerning God's image under man's commonplace. Why cannot

I do the same? There it is, beneath the slouching gait, the dull eyes, the boorish tongue, the uncouth manner, there lies God's image, asleep, yet ready to be wakened into beauty. Why cannot I awaken it, as Christ did, with the kiss of love? Ah! it is because I have not the heart of love. It is because my eyes are veiled with pride, and my lips frozen with egotism. Forgive me, forgive me, thou royal Jesus! Forgive me, and help me to climb up into thy kingly humility, that sees, and understands, and loves the most commonplace things, because itself is not commonplace.

# XVI

## ON HARDSHIPS

I LOOK back over the years thou hast
given me, my Father, and though
the happy days are sweet and many, it
is the days of hardship that I remember,
and remember to bless. In them thou
didst teach me thy waiting strength. In
them I drew close to thy love. Through
them I came to rise above the frets of
time and to know the joy of immortality.
They interpreted the world to me, and
myself to the world. Thou hast fed me
with rich hardships, and I have grown.
And how patient thou hast been with
my petulance, as I flung out my arms
against thee in the night, and buffeted
thy wise designs in the daytime! Thy
corrections have been few for such a
peevish child. And what shall I think
of the worries that now harass me?

Shall I learn nothing from the past, but continue to fight God's leading? O thou Shepherd of men, well do I know these sharp grievances to be but the brambles thou hast set to keep my feet from straying, and the disappointments and failures that vex me are the pressure of thy restraining hand. Knowing it, may I live that knowledge! May joy sing on my lips, and peace shine in my eyes, and the faith that never fails dwell in my heart. So may I walk with thee through the lights and shadows of the world, and know no darkness.

# XVII

## ON JUDGING OTHERS

MY words were true, and the rebuke was needed; and yet I am
ashamed that I gave it. I gave it in
humility, conscious that I might sin in
the same way; yet I repent as if for
pride. Why am I afraid to deal frankly
with my brothers? It is not fear of
them, but of myself. For, though I invite criticism, my heart fights against
it; and though I am sometimes brave
enough to give it, I am never brave
enough to receive it. And what right
have I to impose on others a burden I
shrink from? Yet it should not be a
burden. How much I might help my
friend by telling him of that one fault of
his! How greatly I need to know my
own! I should not be unkindly silent
simply because he may misjudge my

motives.   Judge ?   Ah, who was it said,
" Judge not " ?   I have been judging my
friend ; in humility and lovingly, yet I
have judged him.   And I myself would
not be judged with that judgment, save
by the all-seeing One.   Help me, thou
pitying Judge, to help my brother and
be helped by him, humbly leaving with
thee all decision on our lives.

# XVIII

## ON LONG GRIEF

THE old grief again, the same as yesterday, bitter as when it burst upon me months ago. My prayers have not lessened its anguish, and the consolations of religion have not softened the hardness of it. The very cares and perplexities of this world are kinder to me, for they make me forget it, until it rushes back upon me in some quiet hour when I have time to think. O God, is it thy will that I should be pursued by this grief through all the years of eternity? In man is no help; is there none in thee? The peace that in all things else thy Son's religion gives me, in dealings with men, in turmoil of business, in studies and in friendships, — is this peace to fail where I need it most? Or at least where I wish it most.

For thou, O God, dost know my need. In all things else I can see that thou hast known my need. Shall I not trust thy hand at this one point of darkness? From thine own Son thou didst not remove the bitter cup. Thou didst press it to his lips when his soul cried out in anguish. Shall I ask thee to spare me? I will bless thy name that my grief is but one. Though it is heavy, I will bless thee that it is no heavier. If it be thy will that through all eternity this grief shall be my comrade, grant me grace to say, Father, thy will be done. There is no lack of love with thee, and thy love has no lack of wisdom. Thy loving will be done.

# XIX

## ON THE BIBLE

HOW shall I read aright in the book of the law? My brothers speak of unfailing joy in it, but I cannot ·say that. My sisters seek it with a hunger and a thirst that I do not feel. I remember hours when its strong words have borne me up to God's throne, to the city of peace, to the river of life; but I remember, also, many an hour of level reading that lifted me no fraction from my worries. Why art thou not always with thy book, O God, or with thy servant when he reads it? Yet, hold! What am I to chide God, or chafe at his withdrawal, or set the hour of his coming and the length of his stay? Mine it is to seek him ever in the ways of his appointing; and his it is to make me conscious of his nearness when he will.

Mine it is to be grateful for the visions God has shown me, to count one hour of grace from his book enough, and honor it forever for that hour ; his it is to crown my gratitude with higher revelations, and bless the obedient eyes with sweeter visions.    Make me willing, my Father, for one pearl of great truth to sell my days and nights.    Teach me to prize the Bible I know, that I may come to know a holier one.

# XX

## ON TRIFLES

WHY can I not separate the essentials of my life from the nonessentials ? Here I am as gloomy over the peevishness of a subordinate as I would be on the death of a friend ; and yesterday the failure to have my own way about a trifle made my whole lifework seem darkly ruined. What avails my heirship of eternity if I shuffle along, the slave of time ? What avails it that the King is my Father, if every worldly worry is my master ? What avails it that my mind can look before and after, if its clownish, timorous gaze is fettered to the clay I walk on ? Men have gone about their duller tasks more faithfully than I, have met with more compelling vigor the prosaic foes of humdrum toil, and yet have kept calm spirits through

it all, and never have ceased to hear the
songs of angels. Instead of disagree-
ments with well-meaning friends, others
have borne the bitter rush of foes. Instead of backward eddies in a swiftly
prosperous stream, others have had to
breast opposing waves, and never have
known success. They were more blest
in their woes than I in my blessings.
Ah, my God, I deserve the lightning of
thine anger! Well might it turn my
fortune into curses, my friends into foes,
and my peevish fuming into sorrow with
cause! But spare me in thy mercy as
thou hast spared me. Grant me the
wisdom to know my happiness, wherein
it lies. Help me to the strength that
holds on to thee. Help me to the sane-
ness that sees things in their right proportions, and to the peace that all earth's
turmoils cannot shake. For thou, O God
my Father, art health and peace, and
the help that never fails.

# XXI

## ON THE LOSS OF CREDIT

THAT was a good piece of work, and he got the credit for it. How often this happens to me, that others are praised for things I have done, or at least made possible for them to do! Why should I continue to labor, while others reap my reward? An unjust and unwise world, so blind to men's deserving! Could not God render to every one his reward according to his deeds? — Ah, faithless wretch that I am, he has promised to do that very thing! What reward do I profess to seek, other than his approval? What reward do I really seek, other than men's approval and my own? O thou who didst say of such as I, "They have their reward," save me from self-deceit. I deserve the misunderstanding of others, I who am so insincere with myself.  O Christ, who didst seek recognition for thy work only that thy Father might be recognized in it, teach me the like zealous humility. Show me how much credit I, too, am getting for things I owe to others.  Help me to prefer my brother's honor to my own.  Teach me rather to dread undeserved praise than to seek the praise I deserve.  Grant me wisdom to lose all thought of what I have done in shame at the pettiness of it, when measured against thy plans, and thy mighty, everready help.

# XXII

## ON ENVY

WHY must I envy all excellency in others? What should it be to me that this one makes beautiful music, that this one is a strong orator. that this one, again, is shrewd in handicraft? It is well to admire others; but this is more than admiration, because it makes me miserable. It is well to be ambitious; but this is less than ambition, because it makes me weak. This orator — is he skilled in music? This painter — is he a good mechanic? These all have their one gift, and I have mine: why should I long for theirs? What should theirs be to me but an added joy and pride? Is not the Lord of all talents with theirs as he is with mine? But ah! is he with mine? He cannot be with discontent, half-hearted zeal, and

glances cast aslant.   He cannot remain
with gifts so gracelessly received.   O
God of my talent! teach me how to use
it.   I would be so filled with the joy of
it that I have no wish for other gifts ; so
firm in loyalty to it that other allegiance
would be impossible.   Then I shall praise
thee for the talents of other men, when
I have learned to praise thee for my
own.

# XXIII

## ON PITY

I ENDURE too complaisantly the sorrows of others. The pitying word is ready, but not always the pitying heart; and when my condolences do not cheat me, I wonder if they ever deceive another. Is not sorrow too sad a thing to be saddened still more by hypocrisy? If my heart is not tender, is it well to soften my voice? And then, the wretched selfishness of it: when a petty worry of mine dulls my ears to a neighbor's calamity, and a pain in my finger occupies me more than his loss of his child. Is this loving my neighbor as myself? O Christ, thy way is hard, thy precepts are high, I cannot attain to them! I grovel in my mean and petty self-love, which is hateful to me, yet I am ever slipping back into it. Have

45

pity upon me, with that pity which I grudge to others. Strengthen this weak sorrow of mine, that it may spend itself away from itself. Thy woe upon earth was greater than all earth's pain, and it was woe that men bore so lightly the pains of their brothers. Forgive me, O Christ, that I thus grieve thy heart. Forgive me, that I thus mar thy image in myself. And teach me, that serving others after thine own blessed way, I may lose, in the divine sorrow of sympathy, the sorrow and shame of my unfeeling heart.

# XXIV

## ON GLOOM

THE God of joy bids me be happy, yet I let my heart be troubled. My mind tells me that gloom is sin, and straightway cheerlessness condemns me. Friends, a host of them, will be encamped around me ; above me will float the banner of love ; the work of my hands will be prospered ; yet my life will be so sadly poised withal, and inclined away from what is sane and peaceful, that the lightest touch of the finger of failure will overturn it into the Slough of Despond. O Christ of Cana, how may my life be a feast ? O thou who dost flood the universe with the light of thy sun, shine in my life, not now and then, but forever. I am weary of joy's uncertainty, of the peace that is fickle as a desert stream. Grant me thy peace that floweth as a river, thy peace that recks not of its peacefulness, thy joy whose essence is the joy of others. Make me so busy with useful work that I shall not feel the touch of the finger of failure. So breathe into me the energy of thy strong purposes that I shall not need to sit at a feast. Help me to such pity for the trouble of others that I shall be careless whether my own heart is troubled or not. Let thy joy be in me, that my joy may be fulfilled.

# XXV

## ON WORSHIP

I PROFESS with my lips a love for the courts of the Lord, but that love is very languid, and easy to be refused. This half-willing church-going cheats men and cheats me, but it does not cheat God. He knows when the heart stays at home. And yet I would not wait to be willing to go to the house of the Lord. Yesterday I went with slow feet, but they bore me to the gates of heaven. Many and many a time God has thus shamed with a blessing my wandering desires. Surely his sanctuary has light even for half-shut eyes, and God's music reaches even to listless ears. Surely God will be pleased if even by grudging attendance I say, "Lord, I am willing that thou shouldest help my unwillingness." But will he be pleased

if, as for so many years, I remain satisfied with my unwillingness? How can
I come to love God constantly, with such
fickle love for God's sanctuary? Nay,
is it not, rather, that I will love God's
house more when I have come to love
God more? Forgive me, Father, that I
have so often dishonored the Holy Spirit
by regarding the eloquence of men, the
harmony of human choirs, the imposing
throng below and rich roof above, rather
than thy eloquence and beauty, and the
singing of thy peace. Teach me to
know with the life what I now know
with the mind, that the secret of joy in
worship is love of God and service of
men.

# XXVI

## ON UNSELFISHNESS

WHEN I drive out thoughts of self
with thoughts of others, my joy
comes in with their joy. When I go
about doing good, my sorrows stay at
home, and all gladness runs to find me.
On such days my worries hide away,
my failures and disappointments are forgotten, my eye looks brightly upon the
future, what time it is not entranced
with the present. Such seasons have
been mine, my Father ; and yet, O what
a stupid scholar I am ! I turn from what
I have found so pleasant, and seek the
old, sad ways of selfishness. Is it a dis-
temper in my blood, a madness in my
veins ? Is it in punishment for my sins,
that though I know happiness I flee from
it ? O God, I am wrong at heart ; my
instincts are not pure, they are not safe

guides; leave me not alone with them. I need thee every hour, my judgment is so weak before the spirit of evil with which I contend; my conscience is so easily entreated, and my will led captive by misery. Lord, I will be glad that my instincts are untrue, for their treachery shall lead me to trust in thee.

# XXVII

## ON COWARDICE

A CRAVEN disciple, a faint-hearted follower, a cowardly Christian! What will my Lord say to me in that day when he speaks his praise and utters his terrible blame? I have heard Christ reviled, and my silence condemned myself more than it abashed the blasphemers. I have listened to skeptics parading their wilful doubts, and my faith has been as mute as unfaith. When testimony to God's love and power has been wanted, my lips have been dumb. When others have been tearing down the idols of error, my hands have hung by my side. Where witness-bearing was easy and to be applauded, I have lifted up my voice. Into places where men scorn the name of Christ, into drunkards' dens, the

hovels of outcasts, prisons, and haunts
of vice, I have not gone. What sacrifice
have I made for thee, O Christ? What
hardship have I borne for thee, O Christ?
What indignity have I suffered for thee,
O Christ? And thou hast loved me.
And thou hast heaped thy kindnesses
upon me. I am rich in all things, ex-
cept in service. I quiet myself with the
thought that no chance for heroism has
come; but it has. I quiet myself with
the thought that thou hast called others
to these tasks; but thou hast called me.
I persuade myself that at some future
time I will do thy will; but I will not,
because I am not about it now. As thy
apostles of old prayed to thee for boldness, so do I, out of my craven fear and
indecision, O Lord, Christ of Gethse-
mane! Grant that I may speak thy word
with all boldness, while thou stretchest
forth thy hand. And as thou didst shake
their meeting place, in testimony of fulfilment, shake thou my very life from its
foundations, if thou wilt. Lift my spirit,
O Lord, into thy places of power.

# XXVIII

## ON AN ERRING FRIEND

WHY does the discovery of that fault in my honored friend chill my faith in man and God alike? I have been seeking perfection in the sinful, and wisdom in the fallible. I have made an idol of the creature, and God has mercifully overthrown my idol. Shall I be angry with my friend, whose fault has sent me back to God? Shall I be angry with my God, who has made friends but little lower than the angels? Shall I not rather be angry with myself for my foolish estimates both of God and man? I thank thee, Father, for the nobility of my brothers, who with me are toiling at the tasks of the world, fighting against the evil within them and without. Even for their failings I thank thee, so far as in them I see my own heart mirrored, and am led to the only purity, strength, and perfect love of the universe. Grant me a knowledge of thee far higher than comes from thy marred image. Teach me to look upon thy countenance unveiled in its glory. From that sight I shall learn how to look upon my friends.

# XXIX

## ON THE COMING DAY

TO-DAY, if things go wrong, let me consider whether the wrong is within me or without; and if it is within me, I shall not be disconsolate, because then I can remedy it; and if it is without, I shall surely not be disconsolate, because that would do no good. To-day, if I am reproached with any mistake, let me first decide whether I am in error; for if I am not, then I shall be glad, because the reproach cannot harm me; and if I am justly reproached, then I shall thank God for so faithful friends. To-day, if I become depressed, let me examine carefully the cause of my depression; then, if there is no just cause, I shall feel ashamed, but relieved; and if I have any genuine grief, then I shall know that God will come especially near to me to help me bear it. Through this day, O my Father, Satan will press upon me in many forms, but chiefly in the disguise of my own feelings. Protect me from them, I pray thee. Grant my reason such shrewdness and my heart such force of cheer that I shall pierce through Satan's black mists to the secret joy of things. Be with my eyes to-day, that they may see how all is good, in earth and in heaven.

# XXX

## ON SATISFACTION

THERE was I again, urging others
to a life of content, while my own
is poisoned with frequent dissatisfaction;
arguing the Christian's duty of happiness, though my sadness gave the lie to
my plea; even preaching courage out of
cowardly lips. I am not like the Phari-
sees, that lay on others burdens they will
not touch; for I am heavily burdened,
yet counsel others to throw aside their
weights. And this is an added burden,
that I must choose between a faithless
silence and a confession so poorly lived.
This, with all troubles beside, I bring to
thee, thou Burden-bearer. Thou wilt be
displeased as I am with my life, and thou
wilt bid me continue my lip professions
of thee, and so thou wilt not lessen my
shame, but rather increase it; and yet

thou wilt give me peace. Peace in the assurance of thy power, which grows as my weakness grows. Peace in the remembrance that thou knowest in all points what temptation means, and rememberest that I am dust. Peace in the promise of the eternal years, wherein I shall see thee and be like thee, and thus even put to shame my present mocking ideals. I pray thee for grace to see what I lack of the best, and to be courageously dissatisfied. I pray thee for grace to know what my small best is, that I may be satisfied bravely.

# XXXI

## ON NEEDLESS WORRY

THERE are few dark days in my life that do not shine out brightly against the years that have settled about them. Soon, doubtless, these few also will be tenderly interpreted by time. O the long hours, the strength and happiness lost by my feeble faith! O the wasting worries over joys disguised as griefs, and over curses that I have come to bless thee for, my Father! In the growing greatness of thy favor. — no greater now than before, but more clearly seen. — how paltry appear my fretting and my frowning, my needless tears, and my faultfinding convicted of blindness! I have been so impatient with this good world and the good heaven above it. Scornful of others whose minds were skeptical of truth, my own faltering, moody heart has been more skeptical than they. Henceforth I will make the best of life. Nay, I will not ; for thou hast already made the best of it for me ! I will not wait for thy years to disclose the proof of it ; my heart shall know it now. Send what thou wilt, but send with it strength to keep this resolve. My reasoning will not suffice ; I need thy help to be happy.

# XXXII

## ON INGRATITUDE

MY prayers are long wails of petition; they should be anthems of praise. Is my life so meagre that my converse with the giver of it should emphasize its lack, rather than its fulness? Verily, I am needy enough, but my need springs from my lack of contentment, from my poverty of peace and of praise. The crudest catalogue of my blessings should shame me into happiness. I will force myself to the instinct of thanksgiving. I will magnify my goods; nay, they need no magnifying. Rather, my own heart needs enlarging. Who can widen its reaches, out beyond petty worries and mean complaints, into the sunlight of God's love? Who, but God himself? If God be with me, petition need be but a breath, and all the air will be praise.   Blessed Spirit of peace, interpret thyself to me; thy love, and my blessedness.   Help me, that in unwonted joy I may even forget the sin of my ingratitude.   Thou art in the world, drawing it to thyself.   Thou dost plead with me through lips of cloud and flower, with the eloquence of friendship and opportunity.   Thy gates of happiness stand open on the right hand and on the left.   Thou thyself, O Christ, didst pass outside them into my cheerless walks, to invite me in.   Praise to thee for thy love and thy cheer; praise for thy manly strength and thy wisdom thou art ready to give; praise for the power of praise.

# XXXIII

## ON STUDY

THE other day I was downcast at thought of how little I can learn. The sight of textbooks annoys me, and a library catalogue invites despondency ; for there is so much to learn, and I am so ignorant. Things that need to be done, and that I am eager to do, I cannot do, because I do not know enough. The busy years speed mockingly by, and crowd fresh learning into libraries, even while they crowd from my memory what once I knew. Will there not come some happy years, toward the close of life, when I can withdraw from the bustle of affairs, and live in libraries ? What joy to revel in the beauties of old languages, to tread the corridors of the past, and walk through the present world with leisure to see its wonders and come to understand its perfection! What joy to become a scholar, before I die! Yet the world into which I shall die will have slight use for my scholarship. The wisest books will be child's primers there; we shall be turned with gladness from the archives of the past to the archives of the future; the mysteries and splendors of the universe will be our playthings; and all the tongues of earth will seem but savage babble. O Father, if the work thou dost give me to do requires study, I will study, helped by thee; but if thou dost set me tasks that can be done without the lore of libraries, I will not count myself unhappy. Help me to be a student of the things that will not perish, a scholar of the eternities.

# XXXIV

## ON A DISMAL DAY

TO-DAY, while all things are gloomy without, be all things bright within. Let me oppose the peace of my soul to the storm in the sky. Why should these dull clouds of matter, moved here and there almost by the breath of chance, affect my fickle spirit? Is this a nature meet for eternity, when the pettiest things of time can disconcert it? I am serving poor apprenticeship to those constant years. I am preparing little save fret and fume to carry into their smiling serenity. If my temper is at the mercy of a lowering sky, yet more is it speedily soured by a lowering fortune. Nay, so prone am I to this degenerate darkness, so tied to the gloomy elements of this world, that when all the heavens are kind, I make from nothing a shadow for myself to dwell in.  Forgive me, Father of all joy.  Forgive me, Christ of Cana.  Make me ashamed for my childishness, and lift me into manhood. Make me ashamed for the lives my fretfulness has embittered.  Make me ashamed for every spot whereon my shadow has fallen.  O dwell thou in me, and every shadow will be sunshine.  O dwell thou in me, and all my sad fickleness will pass away.  Come to me this day, thou joyous Comforter, and thy joy will be in me, and my joy be fulfilled.

# XXXV

## ON REST

HOW hard it is to rest! Into what should be hours of calm thought, of joyful converse, of prayerful retrospect or prospect, creep reminders of present worries, or fears of coming ill. I know their sinfulness and the shame of it, and long for a happier temper that might give me rest. But no rest comes from within, for there is intrenched the spirit of unrest. A thousand longings are satisfied, and I grieve at the failure of one. A single vacant place means more than a hundred God has filled. The beauty and love that I have, I mourn because I am not worthy to own them; and the beauty and love that I lack, I mourn because they are not mine. I fret in seasons of activity because my work is burdensome, and in seasons of rest because my work is at a standstill. Where, in what school or with what teacher or by what lonely study, can I learn how to rest? O thou who didst promise rest to the souls of the world, come to me in healing quiet. O thou who on thy seventh day didst create rest, thou alone canst give it, and I cannot earn it. Spirit of peace, grant me grace to rest in thee.

# XXXVI

## ON COVETOUSNESS

THOU hast made this world a beautiful world, Creator, Father. Forbid that I should distil temptation from its beauty. Why can I not see green lawns, rare flowers, generous dwelling-places, without poisoning by covetousness the delight of my eyes? Why can I not look upon the river and the wooded hills with gratitude for the glance that should bring peace into my fevered day, rather than complain that it is only a glance? Why do the splendid piles that skill and energy have raised crush with weakening envy my energy and skill? For me the elm has queenly form, for me the pansies have color, though I do not own them. To me the passing glimpse of the forest and the mountain may give a blessing they withhold from

the dweller in their midst. I bless thee
that thou hast given to so many leisure
and a quiet life. I bless thee that such
throngs may live in wealth and ease. I
bless thee that the woods are there, and
the flowers and the ocean, waiting for
my coming. I bless thee that thou dost
sweeten my life with labor, and give zest
by hours of toil to my moments of rest
and delight. Let my delight be also in
my work, and my rest there, too, O my
God. Let it be my coveted luxury to do
thy will.

# XXXVII

## ON THE JOYS OF NATURE

THAT was a gloomy week — the last one. The skies were bright, but I saw only a cloud of black worries. I walked through the sunshine proof against its winsomeness, and moped by myself or snarled among my friends. But this week I have let God have his way with me. I have filled myself full of his beauty and his strong peace. The sweet, silent growing of the flowers has shamed me ; the fresh air has lashed my will to action ; the trees have taught me, as they serve God by standing still ; the army of modest grass-blades has sung me a battle-song. My work has taken to itself something of the energy of nature, and much of its ardent peace. Thy world, O Creator, has myriad messages for me. I need thy help to receive them.   I need thy spirit of unselfishness, that I may leave the cold cell wherein I have shut myself with my frets and my more difficult sorrows, and abandon myself to the majesty and loveliness whereby thou wouldst instruct me. These delights of the natural world, O God, — sunsets, morning splendors, colors and scents and sounds, — are thy ministers, to do thy pleasure.   Thou art ready, I well know, to serve me with them.   O make me ready and zealous to be served.

# XXXVIII

## ON PEACEFULNESS

THE cares of the world throng thick about me. No time for thoughtfulness, no time for quietness, no time for the winning of peace. Longings for heaven are drowned in the clamor of earth, and I am too busy with living to get ready to live. How can one be in the world yet not of it, push through its noisy streets as if he were treading the celestial pavements, hear over its babel the chant of angel voices? How can I win the calmness that passes unmoved amid dangers and walks quietly through all the world's confusion? Ah, possibly I should not have this calmness. Who has told me that God meant it for me? It may be his will that I should have no time for the winning of peace until the rest of death steals upon me; yes, and not even then.  If so, then unrest for me, Lord Jesus!  Then conflict is my peace, and toil is my quietness, and hour hurried on to hour is the best preparation for the eternal years.  In the life thou dost send me I shall best get ready to live.  If the angel voices cannot pierce through its noises, they will sound with a sweeter surprise some day.  If throughout this life my feet must be hot upon earth's pavements, the shores of the crystal sea will be the more delightful.  Thy will be done in me on earth, O Lord, that I may do thy will in heaven.

# XXXIX

## ON MAJORITIES

DO I think that it will not be safe for me to take God at his word until the majority also take him at his word? Am I afraid that "the other things" will not be "added unto" me, who seek first the kingdom of heaven, if my competitors are seeking first the kingdoms of the earth? From this time forth, then, let me cease to compete with my competitors. Let me make trial to-day of the divine partnership. I will forget that I live in a state whose governor is gold, and in a city whose mayor is selfishness. God shall be my state and my city. Dwelling in him, even if it should be alone, I must pity the lonelinesss of all other men. And if, as I go about my work, I am tempted out into boastings and bargainings, advertisement and the counting of heads, what shall I do? Pray; as even now I pray to thee, thou lonely Christ, who art drawing all men to thy loneliness, not that I may be kept from the world, but that I may be kept from the evil in it. Save me, out of a timorous regard for other men, into care for two beings only: thee, and my brother whom I may help to thy joy.

# XL

WHAT a pygmy am I among these immense buildings! How I am lost among these hurrying throngs! Who of these thousands knows my name or cares about my purposes? What will avail the conduct of my life, be it brave and strenuous or weak and ignoble? What matters it whether the raindrop swallowed up of the ocean be a pure raindrop or a tainted one? Doubtless here is need enough, unrest, and ignorance, and misery enough; but so there are diseases among the forest trees: shall the petty ant that crawls over their roots play the physician to the oaks? Doubtless, lost also somewhere among the busy swarms, are other men who, in the love of Christ, are willing to give themselves for Christ's needy; but how to find them, and by what sign to know them? Here are vast enterprises dwarfing the largest designs of the church. Here is power, power in money, in machinery, in men, mightier a thousandfold than all of these powers the church has on her side. Here is a babel of noises, the tradesman, the laborer, the newsboy, the vagrant, the politician, the steam-whistle; and the church-bells are drowned in the clamor. How can the strongest will, the purest mind, the widest love, make an impression on this tumult? Silly egotist, who placed you in this world to make an impression? Who ordained your voice to still earth's babel? Is it not by the many God works upon the many? What can save the world but the obedience of the insignificant? Are not the greatest things, love and duty, possible for the smallest men, in the most hidden places? Do your duty, then, cheerily, humbly, because you are so little; cheerily, proudly, because Christ will work in you, O my soul. And do thou, my Saviour, save me from thoughts of self.

# XLI

## ON RESULTS

ON what am I to work to-day? On wood, cloth, and iron, on paper and canvas? No; on myself, and on my neighbor. And these visible materials, this wood and iron, together with the tools I use, are themselves the tools of my invisible tasks. This much is sure; only it is all so vague. If I could handle the results of the day! If I could count the coin it brings! If I could reckon up my gains as I add my deposits at the bank! Save me, O thou who workest hitherto, from the sluggishness of blinded eyes! Over my ledger, hammer, or needle, I have bent so long that I cannot straighten to see thee above them. But thou canst see me, and canst show thyself to me in them. That presence will dignify them where they were

trivial, beautify them where they were
coarse, fill with romance the most commonplace of them.    And when thou
hast revealed to me the relation of my
tasks to thee, then I shall see clearly
how they affect my neighbor and myself.
If my work does not shrink at thine indwelling, but endures it, I shall know
that my work is true to men and safe for
me.    Teach me, O Christ the Laborer,
truly to know and do my own true toil.

## XLII

### ON TIME FOR WORK

WHY didst thou send me so large purposes, O my Father, with so little time to work them out? Thou hast so touched my heart and crowded my days that as I see more and more that needs to be done, I have less and less time for the doing. O lengthen my days, prolong my years, or else blind me to the need of the world. Grant me an eternity to work in. Indeed, what have I, then? Less than eternity? And what matters it that my eternity will not be on earth? Rather, it would be a dreadful thing to live here forever, since man will not live here forever. And it would be a dreadful thing to have petty purposes, with the eternal years before me. Forbid that the whirl of this earth's eddy of time should confuse me into forgetful-

ness of the eternal years.    Teach thy
hot-headed apprentice an enthusiasm for
thy patient processes.    Remind me ever
by promptings to more than this life can
give me, or I can give to this life, that
my being is to soar beyond these hurried
years and beginnings of tasks, into ages
of  satisfying  accomplishment.    Thus
may my  common  days  be  mated  with
eternity.

# XLIII

## ON HEROISM

WHEN I read of the heroes of old,
I bow my head in shame. Was
it for such as I that they sang in the fire,
preached joyously in prison, faced lions
with a smile? What gain to me from
all their heroism if I am to go through
life shrinking before human disapproval,
covetous at sight of others' good, and
weak with disappointment and discontent? What boots it that I know the
way of heroism if I do not walk in it, or
that I admire the brave if I do not imitate their bravery? I count men's words
of praise as a miser counts his coin. I
lose the good I have in longing for other
goods. My desire to help men falls
down dead at shock of a discourtesy.
And so falsely do I train my inclinations
and my feelings that those circumstances

seem most material to me which my reason tells me are most immaterial, and
the essentials of happy usefulness are
tossed aside. O thou who didst create
men and their world, and who with all
thy loving nearness to us art so inde-
pendent of us, grant to me, thy creature,
something of thine independence. Be
thou my satisfaction, my sufficient praise,
my ease, my goods, my world. Teach
me that if I regard thee, I need not regard men, save with the brave love
wherewith thou dost regard them, — the
love that gives, but does not require.
Help me to be so much thy creature,
my Father, that I may not be the creature of thy world.

# XLIV

## ON HIDING SORROW

IT was only a moment's trouble, soon to be chased away by work and pleasure ; but I named it as I left my dear ones, and darkened the day for them. Why do I thoughtlessly force others to share my sorrows when they cannot share their transformation into joy? Nay : why not give others my joys, and keep my sorrows to myself? I want sympathy, and my dear ones want to give it, that is true ; but their sympathy will find calls enough from griefs and pains I cannot hide ; let me not weight it overmuch. It does not lighten these petty worries to thrust them on others' shoulders ; I merely add to my own the burden of shame and remorse. Let me, rather, hide bravely my troubles when I can, and lighten them by lightening the load of some dear one. Does not the Bible hint to me that I may best bear my own burdens by bearing the burdens of others? Dear Lord, how often my querulousness magnifies a cloud no larger, to my own life, than a man's hand, into a blackness that covers all the heavens for those who love me! Dear Lord, could they know, as thou dost know, how lightly rest upon me these troubles of mine they take so seriously! O Christ, who on earth didst never parade thy sorrow, but even at its deadliest withdrew it under the dark olive-trees in the Garden, teach my tongue fit silence from its little frets, that thus my heart may come to disregard them. Teach me to exhibit my life to others in its just proportions, not sadder than it is to my loved ones, and sunnier than it is to all beside. So, when great sorrows come, I shall have gained strength to bear them, and shall have laid up in my loved ones a reservoir of cheer.

# XLV

## ON THANKSGIVING

HOW grateful I should be to God that his kindness does not cease with my gratitude! Each day that adds to God's unfailing mercies heaps higher the shame of my discontent. The dull earth carries in its heart the stored-up memory of past sunshine and fruitful showers, and shows on its daily face the tokens of them all; but from my duller soul a moment's annoyance wipes away all remembrance of joy. I am ashamed before the blithe stanchness of the trees. The fresh and smiling air upbraids me. The glowing sentences of the Book point fingers at me. I am rebuked by a myriad of bright faces, shining with the beauty of thanksgiving. Thou knowest my life, O God. Thou hast seen me choose darkness rather than light. Thou hast heard my complaining lips snarl at the songs of thy saints. Day after day thy angels of cheer have knocked at my gloomy doors. Thou dost know all my perversity. But my heart is bold, for thou knowest also my sorrow. My shame is no less, but my hope is strong because thou dost see my shame. I can bar thy joy from my life, but I cannot shut out thy pity. In thy great mercy, pitying Father, lift from my life its load of discontent. Win for thyself an entrance into my gloom, and lead me forth. All the wisdom of the world cannot teach me joy. All the power of the world cannot force it upon me. All the happiness of the world cannot shame me to it. Grant me, strong and loving Father, out of thine abundant grace, the grace of thanksgiving.

# XLVI

## ON SINGLENESS OF MIND

I AM so careworn about many things that it is plain I am not seeking the one great thing. Or, if I seek it, it is with the carelessness that lets itself be vexed with other cares. When I hold the overmastering thought of God, I am not held of my worries. When I am directed of thee, O my Father, my perplexing tasks find swift direction, and march in ordered submission. When I have placed thy will first, it gives my will power to control and to accomplish. If my life is troubled, it is only for lack of thy peace. If calls to diverse duties harass me, it is because I have not listened to thy single call. How much time I have lost, blunderingly striving to use thy time! How much energy I have wasted, wrongly choosing my work!

Thou doest myriad deeds where I do one. All the countless intricacies of the universe move in harmony to nicely adjusted ends. There is no fret, no friction, in thy workshops. And thou wilt send to my workshop all this power and skill. O Lord, forgive thy foolish servant, who, like a headstrong apprentice, thought he had learned to direct. Work thy will with me, since not otherwise can I work my will for myself.

# XLVII

## ON OPPOSITION

WHEN my words, meant for right, are turned from their meaning, why am I discomfited? When my plans are opposed, plans that I think God's plans, too, why should I be downcast? When men range themselves against me, me who have God on my side, what is more foolish than anger? O my Father, is it only when I complain of thy providences that I really hold thee all-powerful to work righteousness? I have been dreading what the evil may do, as if thou wert weaker than they. Their words have provoked me, for I have forgotten the thunders of thy judgment. I have feared their designs, for I have forgotten thy counsels. Their harsh glances have embittered me, for I have lost sight of thy countenance. Their anger has filled me with wrath, for I have not set before me thy love. Thou whose honor man's dishonor cannot mar, teach me that it cannot mar mine. Thou whose cause is its own great defence, teach me rather to find safety in it than seek safety for it. Thou who dost not mar with passion or trembling the majestic progress of thy plans, teach me that thy plans need still less either my anger or my fears. Make it my one wish for my work, not that it may not fail, but that it may be espoused by the unfailing One.

# XLVIII

## ON UNSEEN THINGS

I AM living in my body as if I were to live in it forever, and I may be done with it to-morrow. What I shall eat, wherewithal I shall be clothed, how I shall be housed, — such are not fit broodings for one who soon, at longest, will need no food or clothes or shelter, save the full delights of the many mansions. Walls light as a whisper part me from an existence wherein no pain is, no tears, no failure, wherein loved ones know how we love, wherein scholars see swift visions of all truth, and the pleasures we have made for ourselves are forgotten in the joys thou dost make for us, O God of all happiness. The life that now is, rich portal to thy blessed home, I look upon as an abode, and find it cold and cheerless. Teach me, O God, the sane and heavenward look. Why should I fret at any failure here — failure of love or knowledge, power or skill, while the life of full fruition touches my uneasy life at every point, and offers perfect comfort? Only a swing of the great pendulum of eternity, only an instant, as I shall look back on time, and all my heaviest troubles will seem more foolish than my childhood's griefs seem now. Help me, Ancient of days, to live in that happy time, while I work in the present. I am tired of serving the earth; teach me immortality.

# XLIX

## ON REMEMBERING

IT is easy to draw doubt and depression from my past; it is hard to draw from it inspiration and hope. Yet I should win as much cheer from the times when God has upheld me, as despair from the times when I, in my own power, have failed. I cherish in memory my defeats rather than God's victories. A thousand times God has empowered me to do this thing, and still I shrink from it as if God and his tasks had not been tried. Not thus am I to become a veteran of the Lord. Not thus will the fulness of almighty strength, vouchsafed to daily need and weak-winged prayers, be builded into my eternal character. O feeble heart and foolish memory, how many trials and proofs do you need for assurance ? When will you trust the

97

Lord, if not now? Had earthly friend been half as faithful, had mortal father been half as constant and kind, your confidence would rest unmovable on the rock of that experience. Because God is unseen, will you distrust his love, which is seen? Because God does not speak with human voice, will you scorn his eloquent providences? And will you dare to expect continued help from the God whose unfailing power your cowardice denies? O my soul, be strong in the Lord! In sweet remembrance of his comforting presence, in brave remembrance of his upholding, in bold reliance on his forgiveness of your weakness, be strong in the Lord!

# L

## ON CHRISTMAS

THERE will come, some glad day,
a new Christmas, when Christ will
be with men in visible form once more,
to stand by our side, his loving hand
holding ours, his strong voice moving
the rejoicing air, his kind eye piercing
to the hearts of men. I shall have no
more worries, when he comes, for in
him is fulness of joy. I shall have no
griefs, when he comes, for he will bear
all my burdens. When he comes, I
shall be no more perplexed, for his
wisdom is unfailing. All these things,
together with sins and follies and vex-
ations innumerable, will threaten my
Christmas peace, unless he come. Oh,
our Lord Christ, come this Christmas!
Thy weary world is waiting eagerly, and
every Christmas more eagerly, for the

glory and the health of thy coming.
But art thou not here — or why am I
talking with thee? What should matter
the sight of the eye, the touch of the
hand, to one whose eye is soon to fail
and hand to crumble into dust? Art
thou not here, in this room, blessed
Master, as really as ever in the upper
chamber at Jerusalem? Do I not see
thee, with the sight of heaven, and hear
thee, somewhat as seraphs hear? Thou
hast come into my life in clouds of glory,
with thy holy angels. Every day, when
I receive thee, thou dost make a merry
Christmas. So let it be with this gracious season. Open my faithless eyes
and my infidel ears, and teach me to
know thee. Be present in my life as
really as my sister, my mother. One
day with thee, O Christ, as one day with
thee might be, and I think I could never
be alone, and never lack a Christmas.

# LI

## ON FEAR FOR OTHERS

SO many perils are round about my loved ones, — perils of sudden sickness, or of slow ailments concealed from me ; perils of accidents, from the forces of nature, or the forces of man ; perils of long grief, wasting desire, and lost hope; so much of evil that may be coming to them, unseen by me, unseen by them, and inevitable. What can I do to assure the joy of my loved ones, their health of body and better health of mind? What can I do to guard them from malady and myself from loneliness and sorrow? For what should I do without my loved ones? Ah, thou that knowest hearts, how much of this burden of fear is for myself! Yet thou wilt regard the purity of my prayer, and sift its imperfections. Better to my loved ones is danger guarded by thee than safety preserved by myself. Better for them is thy sickness and grief and despair than my perfectings of joy. Yes ; and better for them is my abandonment of them than my fretfulness for them, if I yield them up to thee. Why should I, who perform so poorly the lower care for my dear ones, think of the higher? Until I can make the one day brighter, let me leave their years to thee. Until I have fed more faithfully the common sources of their healthful cheer, let me cease to worry about their long sorrows or long joys. So shall I trustfully carry out the trust thou hast committed to me, and not imperil it by presumption. Teach me, loving Father, to love as knowing thee.

# LII

WHAT is before me in the coming year? God has hidden it from me because I could not bear its sorrows. There are failures as wretched as any in the past, griefs as bitter, longings unsatisfied, ideals unattained. Or if in any way I may grow stronger and happier, a year's improvement will be almost unnoticed. And there are old sorrows that time will not soften, because it has not. I see them lying dark along the way before me, reaching into the black cloud, where they meet who knows what coming dangers and changes and pains? God promises me no better years than he has given me. Indeed, what am I that I should ask for better years? God is greater than my prayers have ever been. God is more eager

than my complaints. If nothing else in
the universe were sure, this would be,
that God has given me all the good I
could bear. Uplifts from many a failure
prove it, fierce griefs assuaged, desires
crowned with fulfilment, and years led
through crooked paths of self-will, yet
ever, by God's grace, to a wider life.
Forgive my weak forebodings, loving
Father. Truly I know that thou hast
hidden the coming year from me, not
because its sorrows are so great, but
because I am not strong enough for its
joys. What wonderful things await me,
back of the sweetly mysterious cloud !
There must be deeper knowledge, for
thou wilt continue to teach me ; and fuller
love, for the years bloom ever the richer
with it : and wider friendships, for my
old friends continually bring me new
ones ; blessed changes that mean no
loss or sorrow, but only the keenness
of joy. I will go forth into the year
with thee, O thou who never with-
holdest !

# One Upward Look
*for*
# Each Day
*of a*
# Month

# FIRST DAY

ON every hand, O Giver of Good, I see the proofs of Thy care for me. This room in which I sit is crowded with reminders of Thee. The objects of use and beauty that fill it, common but wonderful, so many and so varied — how impossible that I could contrive them or deserve them! The very warmth and light that pervade it, the very eyes and flesh that take cognizance of light and heat, the very life that beats in my veins and the intelligence that resides in my brain, Thou didst implant them all and Thou dost momently sustain them. When I begin to think what all this means, what an infinity of minute and loving providences, I am seized with a passion of gratitude and bowed with the shame of my thanklessness. Forgive my unheeding heart, O God. Remind me ever of Thyself, even by the withdrawal of Thy favors for a time, if I forget Thee. For to know Thee is life and to fail of Thee is death, forever. Amen.

## SECOND DAY

O GOD, my Judge, I want my heart to be ready at any time for Thy inspection. I want to keep my life clean, and just, and faithful. I know not when I shall be called upon for the Great Review. It may be to-morrow; it may be this hour. And here are, oh, so many flaws, and impurities, and infidelities! Here is so much failure, and injustice, and sin! Not in years can I cleanse myself and right myself, — and Thou mayst come to-morrow, or to-day, O Judge!

How could I endure it, were not my Judge also my Saviour! Take this poor, unworthy life into Thy hands to-day, Christ Jesus. Fashion it anew, as Thou dost well know how. Prepare it for Thine own coming, yea, for Thine indwelling. I will trust Thee, in this as in all things; and I shall not trust in vain. Amen.

## THIRD DAY

WHAT a blessing is the day's work Thou hast given me, O Master Workman of the universe! I rejoice in it and in Thee. In it, for the exhilaration of endeavor, the exultation of achievement; in Thee, because Thine is the material in which I work, and the strength with which I work, and the far-off, lovely goal toward which my labors tend.

It is a blessing to work with Thee. Working with men and under them breeds so many misunderstandings, so much fretfulness, jealousy, impatience, injustice. But Thou knowest my frame. Thou knowest when I am doing my best. Thou hast patience with my blunders, Thou dost pardon my errors, Thou dost amend my faults, Thou art proud, with a Father's pride, of my successes.

Then let me work with Thee to-day.
Amid all my labor with men, let it be
first with Thee.    Then shall I pass
serenely through the coming hours, and
carry large garners up to eventide.  Hear
me, and grant this prayer for Jesus'
sake.   Amen.

## FOURTH DAY

ALMIGHTY Ruler of the world,
ransom my thoughts, I pray Thee,
from the pettiness that confines them.
How do my prayers wind about myself!
Enlarge me with Thy grand designs for
the nations, Thine age-long purposes
serene and steady.  Let the woes of
mankind put to shame my fretfulness.
Let the vast successes of mankind con-
sole me for my failures.   Let me rejoice
in the wide pleasures of time and space.
I will work none the less thoroughly and
zealously, but as a part of a majestic
whole.   So I shall not be affrighted or
perplexed.   So I shall tread the earth,
not as a hermit, but proudly, as one of

a confident army. So I shall live to-
day — grant it, my Father! — as a portion of Thy will getting done and Thy
kingdom coming. Amen.


## FIFTH DAY

WHY will I let myself be fretted
by men? Why will I allow the
trifles of time to vex me? Father of
infinite space and endless power, I am
Thy son! While I am with Thee, about
Thy tasks, no evil shall befall me. Let
not the fear of evil, which is the sorest
evil, assail my spirit. I will walk through
Thy world serene and confident, for it is
Thy world. Nothing shall affright me,
not even my sins committed, for Thou
hast forgiven them and cast them behind
Thee. Thou wilt remember them no
more forever, and I will remember them
only to praise Thee. And if my own
sins shall not dismay me, still less the
sins of others. Be Thou my peace, O
God, this day and all days, for the sake

of the Lord Jesus, my Prince of Peace.
Amen.

## SIXTH DAY

I AM not sorry that men do not
understand me, when I remember
that Thou, Father, dost understand me
wholly. It is so sweet to have these
secrets with Thee! It is so joyous a
privilege to share with Thee my aspira-
tions, my hopes, my ambitions for this
world, my consciousness of rectitude
when the world misjudges me, — to
know that Thou dost never misjudge
me.

And oh, I am glad that Thou alone
dost know the secret of my sins! Well
for me that others do not see my fair-
ness, since also they do not see my foul-
ness. Well for me that my iniquities
are unveiled only before the eye that is
acquainted also with all my ways, that is
cognizant of my heart's desire, through
all my sinning, for the good.

Thou art my solace, O God. Thou

art my reward, O God. Thou art my
protection, O God. Where no one else
dreams that I need comfort, or deserve
praise, or require a shield from the adversary. Thou alone, dear Father, and
I alone, in blessed, proud companionship, world without end. Amen.


## SEVENTH DAY

I BELIEVE that Thou art in my life,
O God, working with me. Therefore
when I think of Thine attributes, I will
think of them as in my life.

I am not omniscient, but Thou art
omniscient for me. Nor omnipotent,
but Thine almightiness is at my com-
mand. Nor infinitely patient and loving,
but all Thy tenderness broods over me,
and will dwell in me.

My plans stop short with to-morrow,
but Thy plans for me have no end. My
courage often falters, but Thou shalt be
my stay. I am perplexed by many a
dark riddle, but all is clear to Thee.

In Thee I will live and move and have my being. I will trust, and not be afraid. Oh, that I may know Thee, and Thy power ! I will draw closer to Thee, I will rejoice in Thee, I will take to myself the greatest promise of Christ, I in Him and He in Thee. Amen.

## EIGHTH DAY

MY life is full of perplexities and troubles. Whatever way I look, an ominous barrier confronts me. But Thou, Lord, dost see the end from the beginning. Thou art acquainted with all my ways, ways to come as well as ways past. Thou hast prepared a road, however devious, that will lead me around all obstacles, by the side of all dangers, through all difficulties, up all slopes, over all chasms, and bring me at last to a happy home forever.

Thou shalt be my Guide through this day. Thou the chosen Guide of my life. Dissipate my gloom with Thy sunshiny hope. Uphold my faltering progress with the stay of Thy confidence. May I not for a moment forget who is my Helper. It is only when I forget Thee that I am faint-hearted. When I remember Thee, I know that all is well with me, in time and eternity. Praise and honor be to Thy name, O God, my Saviour. Amen.

## NINTH DAY

WHEN ambitious desires seize upon me, seize Thou upon me, O God! Remind me of the King's favor, and upon what it depends. Set before me the King's likeness, how gentle, how lowly, how serviceable! Acquaint me with the glory of the Kingdom, which is righteousness, and peace, and joy. Show me the folly of petty gains, of time wasted upon trifles, of the evanescent applause of worldlings. I would hold myself aloof from it all, as the crown prince from village

wrestling matches or diving for pennies.
I would look far ahead, to the place
prepared, the inheritance reserved. I
would live in the dignity of it, the joyful
confidence of it, the sufficiency of it.
Admit me to this grace, I pray Thee,
my Joint-heir, my Elder Brother. Amen.

## TENTH DAY

O GOD, who in all Thy universes
hast so many creatures, beautiful
and unseemly, active and stolid, helpful
and harmful, but dost uphold the lives
of all and minister tenderly to their
needs, teach me sympathy with uncon-
genial men. As Thou dost descend into
the earth with the mole, and move
through the jungle with the ape, and
guide the fish to its food, enable me to
breathe all atmospheres without disgust,
and to enter all lives with helpfulness.
What am I above the worm, when
matched with Thy height, O Ineffable!
Teach me the humility of Thy Christ,

who took the form of infinite debasement and glorified it into God. So let me move among men, and count it my crown to wash their feet. Amen.

## ELEVENTH DAY

GUARD me, O God, against the unseen dangers of this day. Every moment, from first to last, is open to Thee. It is all a journey that Thy thought has travelled. Thou canst guide me through it because Thou hast been through it. The temptation lurking for me behind some false pleasure, Thou hast noted it. A failure or flaw in my work, it is already before Thine eyes. The friends I am to meet, the opportunities I am to enjoy, the delights that will minister to me, they are present even now in Thy consciousness.

And so, committing myself to Thee, I shall not be surprised by the sudden assault of Satan, nor daunted by failure, nor over-elated by success, nor enervated by delight. I shall become a part of Thy long thinking, Thy large designs. I shall enter into Thy peace. I shall live somewhat as my God lives, dwelling indeed in Him and He in me. May this be my blessed lot, Lord Jesus, to-day and all days. Amen.

## TWELFTH DAY

IT is easy to live a day without thought of Thee, Thou ever-present Christ. It is easy, and it should be impossible. For Thou art always thinking of me. No pleasure brightens my life but is Thy thought made manifest. I win no success that is not the accomplishment of some plan of Thine for me. In the fulfilment of every task, it is Thou that dost work and art satisfied. These many delights of earth and air, these many interests of the busy world that crowd upon me, are all — Thou, Thou! Yet I can forget Thee; for a day or a week forget Thee!

Let not this be my sin to-day, my Saviour, my Friend. Let it not be my sin, my loneliness, and my loss. Cause me to see Thee and hear Thee in every sight and sound, and so shall I come to the day's end in great peace. For I do love Thee, Lord Jesus. Amen.

## THIRTEENTH DAY

MY weak will wanders here and there, it falters before a pebble, it faints beneath a sneer. Daily and hourly, O God, I need Thy fixity of purpose, Thy dauntlessness of zeal. Why should my life, the oak of unceasing ages, bend to the zephyrs of time? My heart is set upon Thee, O God. I have one goal, Thy heaven; one ambition, Thy approval; one unfailing resource, Thy presence and power. Let me not go staggering through this day. Let me not waver at the beck of human opinion. Let me not yield to worldly enticements. My eye is upon Thy face, in this blessed morning hour. Let me not lose the vision in the crowd. As a banner before a knight, move steadily in advance, O Face of serenity and conquest! Amen.

## FOURTEENTH DAY

MAINTAIN me this day, Lord Jesus, in the secret of Thy peace. I do not ask to be withdrawn from men or my tasks, but that Thou wilt go with me, and wrap me about with Thy presence. If harassments await me, Thou wilt await me. If hatred storm upon me, or the bitterness of opposition, Thou wilt make a calm in the midst of the tempest, and place me there. Unknown dangers may be in the day, but a known Safety is in it. Rebuke my petulance and give me grace; my fickleness and give me constancy; my infidelity and give me faith. Fill the day with romance, O Creator! Enrapture me with the charms of discovery — to

know Thee better, and myself, and our
world ! Let us go faring forth, Jesus,
my Guide, and the trees shall sing above
us, and the earth be firm beneath our
feet, and a happy goal shall come in
view before the sunset. For Thou art
my Guide, Lord Jesus. Amen.


## FIFTEENTH DAY

I WILL rejoice, to-day, in the Lord!
My life shall float buoyantly upon
the stream of His providence. I will
catch His sunshine, and reflect it in
merry sparkles. I will put my voice in
tune with the song of creation.

Whatever of doubt or gloom assails
me, I will remember that it is not God's,
but that the world is God's, and life and
death and the great eternity are God's,
and I am God's, and all is well. I shall
know that all is well, and I shall lift up
my head.

This is my hope and prayer for the
day, my Father. And if I fail in faith,

wilt Thou not remind me of Thyself;
by some sharp warning remind me, and
turn me from my infidelity.   For Thine
is the joy everlasting, and Thine is the
truth eternal, and Thine is the happy
life that Jesus lived before men, which
I would imitate this day.   In His name
of light and graciousness.   Amen.

## SIXTEENTH DAY

WHEN the world annoys me with
its fretting cares, speak a quiet
word to my soul, O Christ.   Call me
away to be with Thee.   Without leaving
my tasks, without leaving the throng of
men, may I make the very thought of
Thee a sanctuary.   There receive me
into Thy peace.   There teach me my
eternal destiny.   There lift me above
my worries into the region of Thy calm.
Lay upon my troubled soul the benediction of Thy serenity.   Remind me of
Thy presence with me always, of Thy
power always at hand, of Thy wisdom

ever ready. And send me forth again
from this moment's sanctuary with a
quiet pulse, and a heart confident and
rested. For this blessed communion I
will give Thee endless praise, my Saviour
and my Friend. Amen.


## SEVENTEENTH DAY

I KNOW not what temptations will
assail me to-day, but I know they
will be many, and I know that not one
of them will herald its approach. They
will spring upon me out of ambush.
They will leap upon me when I am
busy with some task, or engrossed in
some pleasure, or wrapped in forget-
fulness.

What shall I do, that I may not be
captured by them? How may I carry
through the day the hatred of vice, the
pure desires, the vision of God, wherewith the morning hour has ennobled
me?

Only by Thy grace in my heart,

Father holy and puissant! I will watch with Thee this day. I will maintain my soul in the thought of Thee. I will not allow things temporal to have dominion over my immortal spirit. I will not become too busy for the possibility of prayer, too merry for the remembrance of danger, too satisfied for the warning of humility. I will hold Thy hand through the coming hours, dear Father; and oh, do Thou hold mine! Amen.

## EIGHTEENTH DAY

IN foolish pride I felt strong in myself, O Thou, my Strength. Forgive my presumption as I mourn my failure. Help me to keep continually framed on my lips the confession, "My strength is the Lord." If I am tempted to forget Thee, as Israel forgot Thee, quicken Thou my memory. When I have tried to walk away from Thee, my steps have tottered as those of a child. Draw me to Thyself in this hour of communion, so

that I may never want to stray again.
Teach me the full meaning of "I need
Thee every hour." Then shall I be strong
in Thy strength, and glorify Thee,
through Jesus Christ. Amen.


## NINETEENTH DAY

GOD of all patience, help me, I pray
Thee, to be patient with myself.
When temptations conquer me, again
and again, help me not to give myself
up. When my endeavors fail, again
and again, maintain my courage and
confidence. When sorrows gather
thickly around me, be Thou my abiding
sunshine. Endow me with Thy perse-
verance. May I never abandon myself while Thou dost not abandon me.
May I rise undismayed from every fall,
rising into Thy loving, outstretched
arms. Not to grow carelessly secure,
resting too easily in Thy forgiveness.
Not to become deadened against sin,
forgetful how Thou dost hate it. But

only to have strength to fight, only to get on my feet again, and yet again, and always again, till in Thy strength and by Thy grace the final victory comes. This I ask for Jesus' sake.    Amen.


## TWENTIETH DAY

I CANNOT leave my work, dear Lord. The cares of the world press upon me, and hem me in on all sides.    But I want to find Thee in the midst of them. I want to come upon Thee, as Thy disciples met Thee in Jerusalem or Capernaum, in some crowd at a street corner, or among the workmen in some shop.    Disclose Thyself to me in Thine own good time and way, but show me Thyself.    Come to me as I am on the point of yielding to the world.    Press back its allurements with Thy nail-pierced hands.    Point me to the waiting skies.    Testify to me anew of the home Thou hast prepared for me.    Assure me of the reality of unseen things.

Speak to my soul with the serenity that calms all its turmoil and the confidence that arouses all its courage. Come near me, be with me, through all the day, Lord Jesus, and bestow upon its close the benediction of Thy peace. In Thy blessed name I ask it. Amen.

## TWENTY-FIRST DAY

THOU shalt be my joy, O Christ; my joy, my confidence, my peace. I will rest my life in Thee. When frets annoy, they shall not annoy me, because I am hidden in Thy serenity. When temptation assails, it shall not assail me, because I am wrapped in Thy righteousness. When sorrows come like the blackness of midnight, they shall not shroud my spirit, because it stays where Thy light shines in a cloudless heaven. Seize me, O Christ, in a resistless, endless grasp! Never let me go, dear Master! Let no smallest portion of my being go, lest it draw the remainder

after it.   I would be wholly Thine, forever Thine, exultantly Thine, O Christ
of Calvary, O Christ of Olivet.   Amen.


## TWENTY - SECOND  DAY

WHAT satisfaction shall I find in
any achievement, compared with
the joy of Thy praise, O Most High?
What pleasure can I anticipate in any
delight of earth, set beside the bliss
of Thy companionship, O Christ, my
Brother?   What danger shall daunt me,
if Thou dost beckon?   What allurement
shall hold me, if Thou dost call?

Alas! though my conscience speaks
thus, my will is feeble, my habits are
chains.   How often I choose the world
instead of heaven, and Satan instead of
my Redeemer!   How often I set aside
my happiness and seek after my misery!

For without Thee, Lord Jesus, I cannot seek after Thee.   Thou must be my
desire, and Thou must be my will.   I
must rest wholly in Thee, even for the

impulse toward Thee. I must be nothing, and Thou all in all. And when thus,
by Thy grace, I become at one with
Thee, I shall for the first time be something, and enter into Thy abundant life.
Grant this petition, O Christ, for Thy
holy name's sake. Amen.

## TWENTY - THIRD DAY

AS I enter upon this day, O my
Father, help me to leave self behind me, and take Thee with me. Nay,
let me not think of taking Thee with me,
but of going forth with Thee, not upon
my tasks but upon Thine. When perplexities confront me through the day,
assure me that Thou also art confronted
by them, and wilt solve them all. When
failures daunt me, make me sensible of
the presence of one who never knew
failure. Leave me not for a moment to
my own devices. Choose for me every
smallest task. Forbid me to think about
myself at all, whether I am succeeding,

how I am appearing, what will be my
reward; and maintain before my mind
the absorbing vision of Thy glory.
Through all this day I would live for
other men and for Thee, as Thy Son
lived, in His power, and for His dear
sake. Amen.

## TWENTY - FOURTH DAY

I NEED no more blessings, Lord. I
need eyes to see what I have. I
need a tongue to sing their praises.
I need a heart to rejoice in them all the
day long.

Thou hast spread the sunshine all
about me, and I have been searching
out the shadows. Thou hast given me
many friends, and I have been glowering
over my few enemies. Thou hast gifted
me with the power to do much and gain
much, and I have rather coveted what
talents I do not possess than used the
abilities I have.

Ah, what a pitiful life I live, gracious

Father! Forgive me, and lift me into
something of Thy largeness of mind.
Take me out of my petty world into Thy
great one. Set me Thy comprehensive
tasks. Bid me sweep one of Thy vast
horizons. Train me in Thy workshops,
by whatever toil, till I have developed,
somewhat, the measure of the stature of
the fulness of Christ. Amen.

## TWENTY-FIFTH DAY

LET Thy grace dwelling in my heart
preserve me, O my Father, from
all thoughts of self that embitter me with
envy, or weaken me with despondency,
or puff me up with pride, or vex me with
discontent. Wean my desires, O God,
from those objects that never can satisfy
them, and fix me on the eternal good.

When I fall, let me rejoice that Thy
purpose has not slipped. When adver-
sity overtakes me, let me be glad that
Thy church is prosperous. In my poverty I will exult, since heaven is rich.

Eternity shall be my time, and the celestial city shall be my abode, beginning on earth, and now.

I will not be cast down, when I might triumph.  I will not be a serf, where I might reign.  Thine be the kingdom, and the power, and the glory.  And Thine is mine, through Jesus Christ, my Elder Brother, my Joint-heir.  Amen.

## TWENTY - SIXTH  DAY

PRAISE to Thee, Thou glorious Creator, for this frame of beauty, this garden of pleasures, this marvellous earth!  I wander in ecstasy through its paths.  The fragrance grows ever sweeter, the flowers more fair.

Thou art not jealous of Thine own work, my Father.  Thou dost not fear for heaven when men love earth.  In every grass blade, in every bit of granite, in every leaf on the trees, I see Thy goodness mirrored.  No least fragment of this crowded creation but has a finger pointing upward. The world is full of voices saying, " If earth is fair, how fair must heaven be ! "

Lord, I will go gladly where Thou callest me, here or there, onward or upward. There can be no lack of beauty or joy where Thou art. The earth is already a heaven, and heaven will have the homelikeness of earth, if only Thou art my heaven within, blessed Lord Jesus. Amen.

## TWENTY · SEVENTH DAY

I AM sinful, but I thank Thee that I know my sins. Daily show me my evil heart, O God !

I am sinful, but I thank Thee that I am struggling against my sins. Be my helper, O my Lord !

I am sinful, but I thank Thee that I know the way toward Thee, my Saviour. Deliver me from evil, O Christ !

I am sinful, but I thank Thee that even my sins force me closer to Thee.

Grant me this recompense out of the shame of them, my Father!

I am sinful, but I thank Thee that I can forget my sins, and go on in the consciousness of a white life. Wash me, O Thou Crucified One, and I shall be whiter than snow. Amen.

## TWENTY EIGHTH DAY

IT is hard to withdraw to Thee from the midst of my thronging cares. Let me find Thee in them, O Thou Blessed One! Thy presence, when I know it, will make a peace in the centre of any turmoil, a refuge of serenity where harshest clamor beats around me.

I will not go where I cannot find Thee. I will engage only in the work which Thou canst ennoble by Thy companionship. I will carry with me the sense of Thy nearness, and O grant that I may never be surprised from it! Grant that lower ambitions may not have dominion over me, but only to merit Thy approval. Grant that petty fears may not harass me, but only the solemn fear of Thy displeasure.

Thus lead me, Christ, my Brother, my God, to pray through all my service and serve through all my praying, and trust Thee and rejoice in Thee forever. Amen.

## TWENTY-NINTH DAY

LORD, make Thyself real to me. Nay, Lord, I would make Thee real to myself. I will think how Thou didst sit by the well at Samaria; and Thou art beside me now. I will remember how Thou didst aid the disciples in their fishing; and Thou wilt help me at my very next task. I will recall how Thou didst raise the widow's son, and with confidence I will lay before Thee the sorrows of my dear ones. Thou wert tempted in the desert, I remember that; and Thou art looking now into my tempted soul, and Thou hast at hand the right weapon against the adversary.

Thou wert there. Thou art here. I see Thee, I hear Thee, I touch Thee, O Thou living Saviour! Blessed be Thy name, that Thou dost come to me, that Thou dost love me, that Thou art eager to help me. Amen.

## THIRTIETH DAY

FATHER, I care too much about men's opinions, and too little about Thine. If a friend has a word of blame, I allow it to embitter my day and injure my work. Let me learn to ask, with each reproof or criticism, whether Thou wouldst lay it upon me. If so, help me to obey it as from Thee, and thank my friend as Thy messenger. If my conscience does not accept it as a word from Thee, help me to go on my way as if it had not been spoken, in love to my friend, and in serene confidence for myself.

I would live to Thee, dear Lord, and not to men. I would serve eternity and not time. I would seek the rewards of heaven rather than the plaudits of earth. Amen.

## THIRTY - FIRST DAY

THOU hast surrounded me with precious human love, my Father, even as Thou hast given me the encompassing air and sunshine. Nay, the air may grow cold and foul, and the sun may pass beneath a cloud or below the horizon, but this love never fails.

How I bless Thee for it! How I implore Thee to preserve my dear ones! Surround them this day and all days with Thy tenderest ministrations. Send the most gracious angels to attend them, for they are so constantly serving others. Hold far from them sickness, poverty, grief, and death. Grant them the peace of heaven's warm valleys. Place in their hearts the singing joy of seraphim. Uphold them in their tasks that are often so heavy, and lighten their hearts with it all.

I am filled with shame when I think how unworthy I am of them, how little time and thought I give them. Forbid that I should postpone love to beyond the Jordan — love and the showing of love. Teach me wherein true life consists, and that my dear ones need less my money than me.

Thou hast shut us up in a house together. May we transform it — they and I — into a very portal of heaven. In the name of Christ, the Lord of my home and of all homes. Amen.

**THE END.**

www.ingramcontent.com/pod-product-compliance
Lightning Source LLC
Chambersburg PA
CBHW021155020426
42331CB00003B/76